the 68 SECOND SPARK

shift your focus, shift your life

Karen Marie

Magnificent Life
Publishing

August • 2015

ISBN-13: 978-0692510148

ISBN-10: 0692510141

To my son and his family,
who are my inspiration!
I love you so much.

Table of Contents

Introduction   6

This World   9

Wants, Desires and Dare I Say Dreams   13

Manifesting   18

Thoughts   20

Belief   24

Details   28

Focus   30

Emotions   34

Energy   38

The 68 Second Spark   40

Sample Processes   50

Journal   63

Good Luck and Additional Tips   65

Thank you   68

"A person is limited only by the thoughts that he chooses."

<u>As A Man Thinketh</u>
James Allen

Introduction

Sixty-eight seconds isn't a lot of time, but if used properly it can change your life!

Imagine if you will a life where your thoughts control everything that happens around you and to you and where you can create whatever your desires are.

Do you know that you are already living that life? Maybe no one ever told you that.

What I'm proposing to you is that you could possibly be just 68 seconds away from manifesting anything that you desire. The 68 Second Spark is the short straight road to get to the desire you want, not the long winding road that may lead to your desire or may lead to a dead end.

Maybe you are on one side of the river and can see your desire on the other side. We can build the bridge to get you to the other side! It can be done NOW! I know that you can do this as I've helped many others do it.

Are you hearing this message clearly? This doesn't have to be a lot of work, just concentrated focus.

I am thrilled to be able to bring this material to you. I am hopeful that you are a possibility thinker like me, and that you read this book with an open mind and continually ask yourself my favorite question – "What if?" What if this could work for me, too? What if I were able to manifest the life I've dreamed of?

I was so excited and could not believe it when I learned about this. I trusted the person who shared it with me, and knew it was working for others. When they talked about it, I was riveted. I knew if it worked for others, it could work for me.

And it did! After I started having consistent success in manifesting through what I have named The 68 Second Spark, I became a believer. Then I started paying attention to people around me who spoke about manifesting and realized that most of them either didn't know about this process, or it wasn't working for them for various reasons.

If you haven't heard material like this before, I am thrilled to be the first to bring this new way of thinking to you. If you have heard about this material in different forms before – that's great. I am excited that you are interested enough to read another resource on this miraculous process.

I will be giving you details that will benefit you. I believe this will be different than how you have heard it before. I will show you step-by-step the way I have been successful with this process with important highlights brought to your attention and caveats of what not to do.

This book is a little book. I specifically wanted this to be a little book because this is a short process.

This thumbnail approach includes all of the elements necessary to be successful. I will be giving some explanations, but by no means will this be an exhaustive resource.

There are lots of other resources available that will cover each step in more depth, but I am giving you enough information to be successful immediately implementing the process.

This book was written to be a quick read, to do a quick process, but don't discount this process as it is very, very powerful.

Have fun with it, and know that you will be successful!

This World

Think about this world that has been created for us to live in. There are many different names for the creator according to the religions of this world. The name may change, but what are consistent on a fundamental level are the basic rules of creation for this world.

Let's discuss what we know about this world. First, and most important, this world was created for us. This means it is never against us. This world wants for us what we want for ourselves.

Let me say that again because this is extremely important – this world was created FOR US, it is NEVER against us.

Secondly, there are no coincidences. Our thoughts create our lives. That means when something happens that we would normally have said, "What a coincidence," we now need to look closer and remember that this world allowed that creation because of a thought that someone had. Was it yours? Was it someone else's?

This world wants us to have everything that we desire and it is that simple. It does work that way. Of course now that we know this, we have to question why we aren't living our perfect life with all of our wants, desires, and dreams.

We actually are, but we don't recognize it. We are always asking and manifesting, but clearly we are not asking in the right way. To put it another way, we aren't following the rules of this world.

The first reality about this world that a lot of people don't understand is that this world has no judgment. Again, let me repeat that because it is extremely important – this world has NO JUDGMENT.

This means that for any thought (positive or negative) that we have and continue to focus on for any length of time, this world perceives that thought as a desire from us and it will respond, working to bring that desire to us.

From this world's perspective, if we are focusing on a thought, it must be something that we desire. The more we focus on it, the more this world feels an urgency for that thought to manifest in our life.

Let's talk a little more about judgment. Because this world has no judgment and sometimes we are feeling judgment about a particular desire, we must realize that this judgment is coming from one of two different places: either from ourselves or from others.

We must pay attention to this because if we are the ones judging what we are asking for, then we are not in proper alignment and there is an incongruency in asking for this desire. If the judgment is coming from others, we need to be certain that we are properly aligned to our desire and that it is not just the desire of someone else.

Let's look briefly at how this works. When we are thinking in a focused way about something for 17 seconds, this triggers this world to think, **"They really want this as they are so focused on it."** That starts the process.

Another reality of this world that we know about is that this world runs on energy everywhere, in everything. Everything has a hertz level, including you.

Having this information allows us to hone our desires further. The rule is that the energy of asking for something has to match the energy of having it.

In other words – if I am asking for the car of my dreams, while asking for it, I must be present in the same energy (hertz) that I will be feeling when I actually own that car.

Another reality of this world is that we can only ask for things that belong to us. In other words, I can't hear someone talking about something that they want and just say, "I want that too."

It doesn't work that way. When we are manifesting things for our lives, our asking must align with who we are at our core.

Example: The car of my dreams is a Cadillac CTS. If I were to suddenly decide to manifest a muscle car, my core would not align with that desire and the energy of my asking could not match up with it.

Wants, Desires and Dare I Say Dreams

Do you want something small or big? How big? Does it change your life, your family's life, or even your whole neighborhood? Does it make a change in your town, country, or whole world?

A key aspect of putting together your wants, desires and dreams is to be certain that you are listening to your inner voice. Our inner voice knows better than anyone else, even us, what is best for us.

Our inner voice comes from the core of our being (I call it our inner being). So listen carefully and remember that you can ask questions of your inner being. It will give you answers.

You have to be quiet enough to hear the answers. How exciting is it that we have an internal GPS that will guide us to the best life for us.

You must be very, very specific when you define your wants, desires, and dreams. In that defining process, the more laser-focused you are the easier and quicker it will manifest. You also must be certain that you have included as many details as you can.

Example: Dream car – A 2011 Volkswagen Jetta TDI. It is black, with a moon roof, leather seats with seat warmers. But when the "perfect car" shows up, it has a standard transmission and you can only drive automatic transmission: a detail you forgot to put into your description.

Let's talk about the dreams that you have for your life. I think of these as the huge wants in my life. These are easy to manifest because they align with who you are at your core.

You should have dreams. They are a basic human need. Do you remember a time when you dreamed of your future and what it would look like? Do you remember being so excited about what you would be doing?

Most of us forgot our dreams years ago. Maybe they seemed silly or so far out of reach that it didn't feel good to even think about them. Maybe someone said our dream could not ever happen.

Some of us even went so far as to tell ourselves we didn't deserve to have that dream or weren't smart enough, or wealthy enough, and so on. Some of us feel like a failure because we haven't achieved enough in our life so far, and we don't even dare to dream of what else could be.

Our dreams are the desires of our heart. They reside in the core of our being. They belong only to us and no one else. I would go so far as to say that you may be the only one who has your exact dream. You may be the only one that can make that dream happen for this world. That's how important your dreams are.

This is why it's critical for us to pay attention. We need to ask this world to help us live out our dreams. They are not only important to us, but may be critical to this world.

I believe if you have a dream that resides in the core of your being, then your dream is possible. It is totally your dream. You know inside you what the steps are to make that dream happen.

Pay attention to what your heart is telling you that you should be doing. What makes your heart "skip a beat" when you think about doing it? Do you want to feed the hungry? Stop abuse? Employ thousands of workers? The sky is the limit, but what is your heart saying?

I am going to guide you step-by-step how to construct a dream that you can then put into a process. As you are going through this process, please pay very specific attention to how you are feeling.

You need to be consciously checking to be certain you aren't having a difficult time with the process. If you are not aligning to it and find it difficult, it could be that the dream that you are defining may not be yours, but actually one that was put into your head by someone else. If it's someone else's dream for you, the dream is not yours.

So, let's make a dream. I can't wait until you see how easy this is.

First, get paper and something to write with. Have it in front of you to take notes. Sit in a comfortable chair that still allows you to write easily.

Relax and close your eyes. Take a couple of deep cleansing breaths and think about connecting to the core of who you are. Ask yourself, "What is my life's dream or purpose?" Just be still and listen.

After a few minutes, ask again. Be patient with yourself. If you've never done this before, you probably don't usually ask yourself questions and get answers back.

Whatever comes up for you, make a note of it. Don't make the mistake of not writing it down and thinking that you will remember it, because often you can't remember later. You may have only one thing come up. Or it could be a few or possibly even a list. All of these are correct.

Now that you have the answer(s) to your question, I want you to pick one of them to define even further.

Close your eyes again and get back into a relaxed state. Take a few more cleansing breaths and ask yourself about the item on your list. Ask yourself to show yourself what this means. What does it look like? Who else is involved?

Keep asking questions. It is amazing what our core will tell us. Just keep asking and keep writing down the answers even if they don't make sense for now.

When you are done with this session, take a break.

Come back to your list. Go through the list and see if you already know within yourself what steps you could take to get this process started. If not, relax yourself again, do your deep breathing, and then ask yourself where to start.

Once you have connected to this topic, make a list of what comes up so that you can make an outline and find a starting point. Now you can use The 68 Second Spark process to move you forward down this path.

Example: You may want to help 200 homeless people find a place to live and employment so they can stay off the street or reunite with their families.

You are going to need a lot of ideas to make this happen. If this is a dream from your core, the answers will come to you. You just need to keep on asking.

Manifesting

I mean manifesting as seeing, materializing, or bringing something into focus. If you want something that you currently don't have, you are asking for it to be manifested somehow into your life.

If it were an object, you could obtain the object in many different ways: You could acquire the money, go out, and purchase it. It could be given to you as a gift.

You could know someone that owns the object and they agree to swap something of yours for it. Or, my favorite way, it will just "show up" in some extraordinary way. I call this "Easy, Effortless."

My favorite part of this process is that when manifesting something, I don't have to give any thought to how. In fact, the how isn't really our business.

I feel we sometimes slow down or stop the process of this world bringing to us what we are asking for because we are looking to receive it through very ordinary means and not looking for the extraordinary ways that this world can actually work.

Remember I talked about how the energy of our asking has to match to the energy of having it? This is very, very important.

In other words, I would be elated to own my Cadillac CTS but I can't focus on it when I am feeling down. I must be feeling elated just like the emotion of owning the car would be for me.

Knowing that you can be 68 seconds away from manifesting the desires of your heart, I'm excited for you.

Thoughts

Imagine a life where your thoughts control everything that happens to you and you can create your desires. What would be the value of a thought then? Immeasurable.

The life we are living is the result of the thoughts we have been thinking. Our thoughts are bringing about everything in our lives. That is why looking at our thinking is so very, very important.

Remember I said this world doesn't judge? That means that we have to be the ones tending to our thinking. It is only this world's function to bring to us what we are "asking for."

We ask by our thoughts. This is the reason that we are receiving the good, the bad and the ugly in our lives. We need to be very attentive to our thoughts. I can't stress enough how vitally important this is to our lives.

Our thinking is the creative process that brings us our desires. Again, this world has no judgment; it is waiting for us to direct it to what we want it to create.

Let's look at an example. Let's say someone falsely accuses me of something with a lot of negative energy coming my way. I could go into anger mode, which would move me into a negative place in my thoughts, and even let it spill outside of me into my words and actions. I would be in a bad mood.

This world is attraction based. Being attraction based means that wherever we are in our emotions, we will continue to attract more of the same until we make a shift either to a more positive emotion or to a more negative emotion.

Going back to the example, if I don't make a shift away from this bad mood quickly, I will be allowing and attracting more negativity into my life.

Think about this in your own life. Think about things that have happened to you and where you were emotionally at those times.

So, in the example, because someone challenged my integrity, I would be focused on the event, on the person and particularly on the words that were said, trying to determine where they came up with this false accusation.

While we feel it is important to analyze this, unfortunately because I'm focusing on it, I'm in a negative emotion, energized by negative energy and bringing more of it to me by the second.

So here's a question for you: While I am in this mode, am I bringing about the desires of my heart? This world thinks so because I'm so focused. But I don't actually want this negative stuff despite my focus at that moment; I want my dream life.

Do you think that during this example I created a negative spark to come into my life? You bet. This world would be interpreting that I want more of the same. Is it any wonder why we may have so much negativity coming into our lives?

Have you heard the saying, "You can't afford a negative thought?" Do you see why that is true? We are manifesting all the time through our thoughts and don't even realize we are doing it.

So everyone is actually already achieving the success of manifestation, but may be doing it while thinking negatively instead of positively. So, let's change it.

It really is this simple:

* Caution – Be very, very careful of the thoughts that you are thinking.
* Again, Caution – Be very, very careful of the thoughts that you are thinking.
* And yet again, Caution – Be very, very careful of the thoughts that you are thinking.

If you keep having the same unwanted things happen to you, you need to pay attention to the thoughts that you keep thinking. Remember, there are no coincidences in this world. Everything happens for a reason.

If you are thinking positive thoughts and you are not having positive things manifested into your life, you need to review your process. When you have thoughts of what you want, ask yourself right then, "Why not?"

You may be in the way of things coming into your life because of doubt or being caught up in how. Remember, how isn't our business to figure out. This world can take of it.

- Have you ever out of the blue thought about a person you haven't seen in a while? They come to your mind and you wonder how they are, what's going on in their life, etc. What happens next? They call you, right? Why? You were thinking about them. You were focused on them.

A quick recap because this is so important to our lives. Our thoughts are creating and obviously controlling the outcomes in our life. So, pay attention to your thoughts. You are creating your world.

Belief

A belief is "an acceptance that a statement is true or that something exists." Or, according to Ester and Jerry Hicks, "A belief is a thought that we keep thinking."

Moving further down this path of thinking, if we want to make a change in our life, we would need to change our beliefs regarding the situation. To do so, we first need to change our thoughts about it.

To make this change, we need to spend time to anchor the thought so that it can become a new belief. This is done with repetition, which builds the belief in both the conscious and the subconscious mind.

Think about what we know about the subconscious mind – it is a recording of everything that happens to us. Because it doesn't have any judgment, it doesn't know the difference between real and fake.

This is why affirmations work. The repetition of saying them makes the subconscious mind believe it and the conscious mind, after enough repetition, stops talking back.

Another way to build a belief is by pointing to evidence of the need for change in our life, logical reasons for wanting the change and even examples of others making the change that you want as well. To make a change in your thought process, you must add emotion and include as many senses as you can.

Let me explain further. When you imagine that the belief you want to change has already happened, add the emotion of having the belief changed. Add as many of your senses as you can to this image.

With your new belief, how would you visualize this change? What would you see differently? Could you hear, smell or taste something related to having now changed this belief? Of course you will feel differently.

Let's say that you want a new job. You have looked around and found the company (let's call it Company X) that you want to work for and you know the position you want to have there (let's call it Director), but you keep doubting whether you would get hired because of the large number of applicants.

You need to change the doubting thoughts (your beliefs). You have to make them concrete. You know that you are going to get the job. That job belongs to you.

First, I would keep repeating the statement, "I am excited to be hired by Company X as a Director." Then as I start feeling that belief, I would close my eyes and imagine what it's like to be working as a Director at Company X. I would imagine that I was walking through the doors of the company as the Director and going to my office. I would imagine sitting at my desk and doing the work.

During this focusing session, I would be holding the emotion of what it would feel like to be an employee doing this work. I would imagine that I looked out my office window and saw a beautiful blue sky, I could hear birds singing and I would feel how comfortable I am sitting in my chair in my office.

I would imagine how pleasant the smell of success in the air is. I would even imagine the taste of a delicious beverage I was enjoying at my desk.

During this time working on the change in your thinking and building your belief, you also want to be "holding space" for this belief. This means that you need to be going through life with the knowledge that this new position is yours.

You are holding the space of living your life with that new job. The job is already yours. You are merely waiting for this world to tell Company X.

Notice something very impactful about this change in belief that we are making. This is not a lot of work. We are merely thinking something new to change the belief and then living as though the change has been made.

Another piece of this is that we need to own the change we are looking to make. We can't be non-committal about it. It is happening, it will happen and it will be so!

This is almost like magic. This is so powerful and simple; it could be embarrassing that we don't have everything that we have ever wanted while we are living our lives in this world.

Think about how you could expand this idea of your beliefs. You can use this in every aspect of your life. It will impact you, your family life, your work life, your social life and, of course, your future.

This expansive idea can and hopefully will change your world. One of my favorite sayings is, "Let's rock your world." Make your life all that it can be so that you can be all that you were created to be. That's exhilarating!

One more thought before moving on: What if? What if what we have discussed is true and it could be true for you and work for you?

What if you do it? Will you use these methods to change your thoughts? Will you use those thoughts to change your beliefs?

Will you allow those changed beliefs to change your life? I certainly hope so.

Details

Details are important. In fact, they are vital. Without the details, our thoughts would cause lots of things we would not want to be manifested into our life.

This is similar to focus but the details are the specifics. I want to focus on this separately because the details are so important.

When laying out the details of your focus, it is vitally important to look at what speaks to you from your core. When you are listing details, pay particular attention if anything is coming up for you from your core.

You need to allow your core to guide you. It will provide you with the why if you are uncertain. You just need to ask for it.

Simply make a list of the details that are important to this focused desire that you have. While making this list of details, be sure to fill in the gaps.

Keep asking yourself, "What's missing?" The more details you include, the more focused you will be when you do the process and these details will provide you with a longer focus period.

As you work through the process, often you will see details unfolding into the desire. Pay particular attention, again, that this is your desire.

Let's look at an example.   Let's say that you have decided that you want to be rich.   You have to clearly define what it means to be rich.

Does it mean that you have a certain amount of money in the bank?   Does it mean that you have a job that brings in a certain amount of income?   Does it mean that you own multiple houses and automobiles? Does it mean that your net worth is a particular amount?

Whichever one of these completes your definition of rich, the process you would go through to manifest each of these would require different details.   Be very specific.

Focus is the key to making this process work.

Focus

You can change your life with the correct focus! Let that statement resonate with you for a few minutes.

Do you understand the power of that statement? This book is about just this concept: you can focus your wants, desires, and dreams right into your life.

Let's talk specifically about focusing. I mentioned being laser focused earlier. So, what does this mean?

Focus is "a central point, of attraction, attention or activity." We are talking about paying attention and having a central point.

When we are focusing on our desires, we need to:

- Be clear, specific and concise;

- Be definitive, accurate and precise;

- Be inclusive: cover the entire scope;

- Be descriptive: include all the information we have about desire;

- Be knowing: confident about what you desire;

- Be emotional: add the emotion of living or living with this desire;

- Use all of our senses: Sight, smell, sound, taste, and touch.

We need this focus to be on a single want. In other words, we can't focus on generally having a better life. This is too broad.

We need to break that down into parts and focus on each one separately. For example, one might want to have more money, a larger home, newer car, a spouse, children, etc. Which of these actually means a better life to you?

Each of these desires would be a different focus. However, in the focusing we don't need to, and I aspire to the opinion that we don't have to, know the how as I mentioned earlier.

If you wanted to have more money, what does that mean? Do you want to have more money by getting a raise at work? Or, is your goal to suddenly have $10,000 in a savings account in a bank? Your focus would be different.

What is your inner core leading you to want in your life? When we are living our life and satisfying our core purpose, the "work" of this is fun, exhilarating and the most meaningful thing you could be doing.

Some call this our passion. Take the time to discover what your core dream is. This will be the key to you living the life that you really have always longed for.

As you are working through this process, it is very important for you to pay attention to every thought that you have, every person you are around, every place and everything that is around you as messages come to us from all these different venues.

Once you start this process, everything around you is working to accomplish this "goal" for you. The coolest part is that everything around you has the power to manifest anything in this world. So pay attention, take notes and be on the lookout for signs, symbols and answers to what you are looking for.

Another aspect of paying attention to everything is that you need to honor the process that you have put into place. When something is brought to assist you in your life, it is very important to honor that and be thankful for all of it. You need to thank your creator for these results.

I'm going to discuss energy in another chapter, but I want to mention it here. There is a lot of energy used in this process. Being thankful, grateful, and appreciative are all emotions that are charged with the highest energy in this created world.

Use that energy and stay in it. It will help you enormously. It is there for all of us to tap into. We just have to be living in that emotion.

Let's take a step back and look at how little work we are doing for this process. We are not really physically doing anything. We're just paying attention at this point.

Again, don't think about the how. Especially don't worry about the how. Just let the process work.

I want to discuss another aspect that people talk about a lot, practice. "Practice makes perfect" is an inaccurate saying. If you practice imperfectly, you will learn the skill incorrectly.

Therefore, perfect practice makes perfect. Keep this in mind when you are focusing because it is very much like practice, you need to get it right.

You need perfect laser focus or you will receive the imperfections that you focused on.

Emotions

We are emotional beings. Some of us may be uncomfortable with emotions, or may have been taught not to speak openly about emotions, but you will need to get emotional to get this process done.

Think how fantastic you are going to feel when you understand this process and it works for you. You will be living every day in the best emotional and most energized place possible.

This process can bring you small desires or big ones. Wouldn't it be cool if you had the desire to live the life you've always dreamed of and you found yourself doing just that. How would you feel?

Emotions or feelings are the sensations you feel in your body when you process an experience. An example that could be rather intense would be how you felt when you experienced the loss of a very close loved one. You probably experienced many different emotions or feelings as you went through the grief process.

When we add emotion to a thought or to any subconscious process, it will produce a better outcome. Whether you are manifesting something new, releasing a habit that's old, or just wanting to feel better I believe adding emotion will give you not just better results, but a home run instead of a base hit.

The way I understand this world, and what I've experienced in my life, is that without emotion behind my request for something, there is no energy behind it. I believe that energy could have created motion and motion is what gets it done.

Think about the emotion of love. It carries a very high energy, wouldn't you agree? Do you remember what it was like to have a new person in your life that you were falling in love with?

Remember being out on a date and staying up very late and still going to work in the morning and doing the rest of your life without "skipping a beat." You were living in that high energy of love and it felt fantastic. Guess what, you had plenty of energy to keep on going and also didn't get sick, right?

Now, just for a moment, think about a time when you felt the emotion of worthlessness. We don't want to live in that energy. It carries a very low energy and feels horrible. Wouldn't you agree? Enough of that.

Just another quick point: Energy attracts energy. So when we are feeling love, we are attracting more love.

When we are feeling worthless, we are attracting worthlessness. So when asking for a desire, we want to be in a place of joy, freedom, love, empowerment or appreciation.

It is very important when thinking about our requests, to link what we are asking for to a higher, more energized emotion. You want to be certain when you are doing any process that you are feeling the emotion that connects you to your desire. It will be a waste of time, emotion, and energy to do any of this work without having this part right.

I think about the relationship between emotions and energy like baking a cake. The dough that makes the cake will remain dough if you don't add the heat of the oven to cook the cake. Once it is cooked, it is complete.

Here is another gem for you. If you are someone that says affirmations, please don't say them if you are not in a positive energy place.

The higher the energy you can be at when you are affirming, the better the chance you will be in a place to receive the affirmations that will help you in changing your life.

Let's look at an example: A childless couple wants to have a baby. The emotions that they have been feeling while going through all the hoops of finding out that they won't ever have a baby, I would guess would be rather negative.

In order to make any manifesting process work for them, they have to focus on the emotions, which will bring the right energy that they will be feeling when they are holding that baby that they have been longing for in their arms:

- Joy;

- Exhilaration;

- Love;

- Peace that it finally happened;

- Happiness;

- Completeness;

- Joined together.

These are all very high emotions. This is the emotional place they need to be to make this happen for them.

Energy

Everything that is in this world has energy: objects, plants, animals, and especially people.

As human beings, our energy levels change depending on the emotions that we are feeling at a particular time. Think about a time when you felt fantastic. Nothing could rock your world, right?

You were vibrating at a very high level. From this place, everything looks positive. We are constantly giving off energy to this world around us. Other people, animals, and plants can feel our energy.

The higher the energy level we are vibrating at, the more positive influence we have in this world. I love the idea that when I am in a good mood, vibrating at a high level, I can make other people get into a better mood.

Just for our well-being and particularly for health reasons, it is very important that we stay in the positive energy emotions. People claim that when we are vibrating in positive emotional energy, it is impossible for our bodies to get sick.

When we stay in positive energy, this energy brings about positive thinking, positive motion to our desires and, of course, an overall more positive life.

Isn't your goal to live a more positive life and have wonderful things happen to you that change your life? Positive energy is the key to making that happen.

Remember, you want to stay as often as possible in those high energy emotions such as thankfulness, love, gratefulness, being appreciative, being joyful. If you are able to stay there, you will literally vibrate yourself into a new life of positivity. I love that!

The lower emotions and all the baggage that comes with them will pass you by. I love that even more!

They can't align with you just like the negative people around you can't align with you. I don't know about you, but I know that this is where I enjoy living.

The 68 Second Spark Process

Just to reiterate what we are doing here (in case you skipped ahead): we can manifest something we desire by focusing on it for 68 seconds. This is very hard for most of us to wrap our minds around.

I personally have been extremely successful with this process and I know of others that have had success with it as well. I am going to walk you through the process that I personally use step-by-step.

While you are doing this process, if you are going to be using visualization, which I strongly recommend, you will be essentially seeing this desire created in your life. Toward the end of your process, you will be watching a few seconds of a movie that shows you in your life with this desire.

You will be viewing this movie with your eyes closed. Therefore, you will be viewing it with what is called your third eye.

The third eye is located in the middle of your forehead above the junction of the eyebrows. Some people believe the third eye is connected to the pineal gland which is a small endocrine gland in the vertebrate brain which produces melatonin, which affects sleep patterns.

When seeing with the third eye, you will see in color, even if you dream in black and white. According to recent studies, 7 out of 8 people dream in color. This number has risen significantly since the 1970's with the introduction of Technicolor movies.

Personally, I know that I dream, but I rarely remember my dreams, and when I do, I see them in black and white. Either is alright for viewing the movie or in visualizing the outcome. I can attest to that fact as I manifest outcomes in my life every day.

To satisfy my curious conscious mind about what this would be similar to, I use the metaphor of a mold being filled up. The mold is the desire that you are asking for, and everything we spoke about earlier in this book is what we are filling it up with. We want to fill it to the top, which is why we need a lot of details.

Our next phase is our want. Our first step in this phase is to double check that we know that this desire belongs to us.

At this point, you also need to check that you are in alignment with the belief that this desire can be yours. In other words, do you believe in your heart that this desire belongs in your life? Can you see yourself achieving and having this desire?

The next step in this phase is the most important. I want you to open up your mind to possibility thinking. Throw away any and all doubting thoughts that come into your head as you prepare yourself to work through this process.

Your belief in this process, or any process you do, is one of the keys to having success. If you have any doubt about this process working, it won't work. You must believe beyond a shadow of a doubt that it will work. If you can't, then you will need to build that belief first.

How do you build that belief? You go back in your life and think of a time when you used a similar process of asking for something you wanted and it worked.

It may have been the bicycle that you just had to have and you thought about it, thought about it, dreamed about it and finally the bicycle was in your life. You need to focus on any and all successes you have had in the past.

This is just an exercise in wanting something very much and then receiving it. It doesn't matter how it showed up in your life.

You can use other peoples' successes for your evidence. You can use me as part of your evidence because I use it all of the time and it works. You are "building a case" for success with this process in your conscious mind.

Now that we have completed the first phase, we will go into the second phase, preparation.

- Pick the place to do your process. I like to be in a quiet place where I can be alone with my thoughts and be very comfortable.

And the last part of this process is like watching a movie, I want to be sitting in a comfortable chair that I would like to sit in to watch a short movie.

- Maybe you want to have some music playing or have a loving pet in the room with you. This is very individual but most important is that you know that you can concentrate, are comfortable and you feel safe.

Very Important – turn the ringer and the vibration off on your phone.

- You need to be relaxed. I do this by taking at least 2 and possibly 3 cleansing breaths to relax.

Your cleansing breath should be held for a count of 2 and exhaled as slowly as you can. After 2 breaths if you are sufficiently relaxed, you can go ahead with the process. If not, take a 3rd cleansing breath. You want to be very, very relaxed to do this process.

- Now you are ready to metaphorically fill up the mold of your desire, to the top if possible, with all of the details. Remember, the more the better.

  Think of as many details as possible. Important details and tiny details are all just as important in doing this process.

  NOTE: If I have more than four or five specific details that I'm going to be using for this process, I'll make a list (that is information going into my conscious mind) that I will have handy for me to refer to as I'm working through the process.

- You want to think of all senses that you can bring into this process as well. Get creative with how you can use each of your 5 senses for this desire.

- Add positive emotions which will bring their energy with them. These are the emotions that are connected to having this desire present in your life.

Ramp it up. The higher the emotion, the higher the energy. How will you feel when you have this desire in your life? Experience it!

Next are the steps that I use, from the place where I am after doing the preparation steps discussed above. I am now going to do the work. This is **The 68 Second Spark process**.

* If you like, you can start a timer. I use the stopwatch on my phone so I can check my progress later. If using a timer, even though I am starting it now, the 68-second count won't start until all of the pieces are in place to achieve the desire.

    For me, I know exactly when the 68-second count would start as when I have arrived at the place where I am manifesting my desire, I feel like I am flying. I feel limitless! This feeling is throughout my body and for me, there is nothing else that feels this way.

    This feeling or this knowing piece is different for everyone. You have to figure this one out for yourself, but I guarantee that you know when you have reached the manifesting place.

- My eyes are closed and I put a picture in my mind's eye of my desire. I notice each of my senses and what they are bringing to me. I listen to any and all noises in the room. I smell the air and take note of any and all odors.

- I touch something important to me (I always wear a piece of jewelry that has special meaning to me and it has an energy stone in it). I think about the taste of eating something very enjoyable to me to get my salivary glands working. All of this is happening while I think about my desire.

- During this first step, my emotions have already been ramped up but often for me, and most people, emotions are felt in only one place in my body. I expand that feeling until it is flowing everywhere in my body, from the very top of my head to the tips of my toes. I am bathed in that emotion. At this point, I am usually flying.

- Because I am at that place, now is when the countdown to 68 seconds would begin.

- I am very auditory, so from this place I say out loud the desire and each of the details that I put into my mold. I stay laser focused on each detail as I say them and I do so at a normal pace. I emphasize the important words for me. I say these several times because I am very auditory. Again, I am engaging both my subconscious and the conscious minds.

- I stay in this place as long as I can.

- When my mind wanders away, the focus time is up. I check my phone to see how much time has passed since I started the stopwatch. I just guess how much focus time I achieved. If I am short, I go back and try and figure out where I can extend the time.

NOTE: For me, every time I have achieved the 68-second mark, I know I did. It is a feeling of knowing that it is done. For me it is a feeling of completion.

I look at the process like we are climbing the ladder of manifesting.

The manifesting ladder only has 4 rungs: 17 seconds, 34 seconds, 51 seconds and the top rung is at 68 seconds: our goal.

This is how I believe this world sees our focused desires:

- If we focus for 17 seconds, then this desire is out there and this world is aware of it.

- If we focus for 34 seconds, then not only is this world aware of it but it has begun the process of bringing this desire closer to us.

- If we focus for 51 seconds, then the desire is moving more rapidly towards our life.

- If we focus for 68 seconds, it is right around the corner, if not right in front of us. At this point, I believe it has been manifested and it will show up quickly.

  I stay focused on everything around me, looking, watching and waiting with anticipation for my desire as I know it has been manifested and if it is an object, it is mine.

If you didn't make it for the full 68 seconds, try again. Make certain you have all of the pieces together and try it a few more times.

For me, after trying it for 3 or 4 times, I will take a break and go back to the process either later in the day or the next day. In the meantime, I will think of other details that I can add to keep my mind single-focused to get the time to 68 seconds.

NOTE: Once I have achieved this desire, if I made a list of details during this process, I not only will document it in my Evidence Journal, (covered in the Journal chapter), but I will tape that paper into my Evidence Journal as well so I remember all the details that I used for this manifestation.

You now have all the tools you need to do this process and to change your life. I have helped many people through this process and you too can be successful using this process.

Follow your intuition! There may be things that you add to this that will help you be more successful. There may be parts that I have offered that for you aren't lining up.

Each of us is a unique individual and this is just an outline. You need to find what works for you.

When you are using your imagination, you want to get as specific as possible. Use your imagination as a tool for you in this process and in your life. I am awed daily by what people come up with in their imagination.

I have found in working with clients that sometimes the single-focus needed to accomplish the manifestation of a desire is difficult and after many attempts, the outcome still hasn't been achieved.

Then we change the process to be like a mini movie and even though it is not single-focused, I believe this works because it is a lot longer and allows people to have more emotion. Everyone loves a good movie!

Sample Processes

The 68 Second Spark examples I am going to offer here are the actual processes I would use that start with the same pre steps to make the mini movies that I referred to earlier. These processes pick up after the preparation work has been done.

Just to review, this is the preparation:

Step 1: Believe
Step 2: Be in a quiet, safe place
Step 3: Sit in a comfortable position
Step 4: Take cleansing breaths
Step 5: Visualize all details
Step 6: Add the Senses
Step 7: Add emotions charged with energy
Step 8: Now start the process

Better Relationship

The premise for this process is that there is a friend, relative, or possibly even a co-worker who is very negative. Every time they speak, negative comments come out of their mouth, which makes it frustrating to stay in a relationship with them. Because of this negativity, it is very uncomfortable.

Details:

* Change conversation from negative to positive

* Change their perspective so they can see a situation in positive way

- Having lighter conversations and they can now speak positively about events and people

- A positive personality

Senses:

- Hear the words

- See her body posture and her hand movements while she talks

- Smell her perfume

- Taste the french fries that we enjoy in the cafeteria together

Emotions charged with energy:

- Excited to be helping her to change

- Happy that I won't have to listen to negativity any longer

The mini movie I'll play:

I am at home and the phone rings.

It's Sabrina on the line and I am dreading speaking with her because there is always something negative that she's calling me to complain about.

But I decide as I pick up the phone that I will stay in a positive mood and I will continue to do my best to allow her to see the positive in whatever drama she has going.

I hear her say, "I'm calling because I just spoke with my mom and she isn't feeling well, as usual. This has been going on for a few months and I told her to go to the doctor, but of course she never takes my advice."

I can just imagine Sabrina's body posture as she gets this certain stance whenever she is getting very upset and I can see her hands moving about as she speaks.

She goes on, "Can you believe it, she made an appointment for the day after tomorrow but doesn't want to go alone because she is afraid of what her doctor is going to tell her. She asked me to take a vacation day so I can take her. I can't believe that she can't go herself. Give me a break. My mom getting older is really starting to become an inconvenience."

I hear myself say to Sabrina, "I'm so sorry to hear about your situation with your mom, but the good news is that you have plenty of time off due to you from work. And you have an excuse to miss office clean-up day, you lucky girl! To top it off, you get to spend the day with your mom. I wish I had time off to be able to take my mom to the doctor."

Now it is three days later and I see Sabrina at work and as I approach her, I can smell her perfume and I remember how she felt needing to take her mom to the doctor. I am hoping that she has reframed it and was able to enjoy their time together. I wish the very best for both of them.

I hear myself saying, "Hi Sabrina. How is your mom?" Sabrina starts to smile and is very excited as she says to me, "I am so relieved. The doctor found out that the issues she was having were caused by a side effect to a liquid supplement she was taking. He said that her body became unbalanced. Can you believe it? We are all so relieved."

I hear myself say, "Sabrina, I am so happy for your mom and your entire family. I can see how relieved you are and I'm so glad that you are smiling again. You look lovely when you smile."

Then Sabrina says, "I know, I feel like we have been given more time to be together and I am thankful for that." She continues, "You know, lately it seems like more and more positive things have been happening to me. I know you have been telling me that I should be more positive and I think it is working for me. Thank you for pointing this out to me. I believe it is changing my life and the life of the people around me."

I hear myself say, "You are very welcome and I am so excited for you to see life through a more positive lens. I've got to get back to work, but I'd love to catch lunch this afternoon in the cafeteria to hear more, if you are free." We agree to meet for lunch.

As I walk away from Sabrina toward my office I see Sabrina smiling from ear to ear and I am excited to be meeting her for lunch. My salivary glands kick in as I can just imagine the taste of the delicious french fries that we will share together at lunch. The only time I have them is when we lunch together and I am excited to talk with Sabrina more and enjoy delicious french fries.

I feel fantastic that I could make a positive influence in her life. I know that she is on a better path and I am so thankful that I could help her to make this shift in her life.

Purchasing a Reliable Car

The premise for this process is that my car is no longer reliable and needs to be replaced with a newer one. Shopping for cars can be unpleasant as people aren't always honest about their vehicles, especially older ones, and dealers may not always give the full story.

Details:

- I want to purchase a 2010 Toyota Camry

- I can afford $11,500

- I need a car with 4 doors

- I want tinted windows

- I want it to be reliable

- New brakes and tires

- Would like an XLE model

Senses:

- Hear the words of the owner describing the car

- I see the car

- I smell how clean the car is

- I feel how good the car rides

- I run my hand over seats and feel that they have been taken care of

- I imagine how great the ice cream will taste the next time I get an ice cream cone and eat it in my new car

Emotions and Energy:

- Thrilled to have a newer car that is reliable

- Excited that I found one within my price range

- Freedom that I can drive wherever I need to go and I don't have to be concerned about my car

The mini movie I'll play:

I'm at home searching on the computer for used cars. I come across the local Craig's List ads and realize that there are 3 vehicles listed that I believe could be what I am looking for.

I go over the pictures and have chosen a private party to call. This one is the really nice gray color that I like. The asking price is $14,000.

I dial the phone number listed and a man with a very pleasant voice answers. I ask him to tell me about the car and he says that he purchased the car new from XYZ Toyota right down the street and that all of the maintenance on the car has been done by them. He has really enjoyed driving this car and it sounds like he has taken very good care of the car too.

I watch myself on the phone and I hear myself ask him why he is selling the car. He says he is very, very lucky and just won a brand new Camry. I can just feel the excitement in his voice about his luck. I see myself change my posture slightly as I ask him whether his price is negotiable. I hear him say, possibly. Why don't you come over and test drive it and we can talk?

I hear him giving me directions and I am writing the address and directions down on a piece of paper. I am so excited!

Now I continue to watch as I go out to my garage, get into my 2000 Camry, back the car out, close the garage door and drive to the address he gave me.

As soon as I approach the house, I see the car in the driveway and I know instantly that it is the right one for me. I am really feeling excited now! I am hopeful that we can come to an agreement on the price.

I meet him and see myself looking over the car very carefully and can feel the anticipation of taking the car for a test drive. I have opened all of the doors, looked in the trunk and gone over all of the features and I realize that it has everything that I wanted and much more. It is a 4-door, it has tinted windows and it is clean. It looks and smells so clean. I've never seen a used car that looked so clean.

I look at the tires and they appear to be brand new. I hear myself ask him about the tires and I hear him respond that, yes, you are very observant, the tires are new, just 200 miles on them. He says he had just purchased new tires, had all 4 brakes done and all of the standard maintenance as he is going on a month-long driving vacation.

I am thrilled that the car is in tip-top shape.

We take the car for a drive and I love how it handles on the road. It handles especially well on the highway. I see myself owning this car.

We come back after the test drive and I tell him that I don't want to have a car payment and I have $11,500 cash that I can pay him for the car.

He thinks for a minute or so and then says, you know something, I won my other car and I only have to pay the taxes on it, so I'm going to pay my good fortune forward and let you purchase this car for $11,500.

I am so excited that I hug him. I am flying so high. I take a moment to enjoy this time as I love feeling this emotion and the energy that comes with it.

I ask him if it would be all right for me to take the car now and he happily says, yes, of course. I immediately call my best friend who lives 5 minutes away and ask if she and her husband can come over to help me drive my new car home. I hear her say, of course, we will. I can hear the excitement in her voice.

They show up minutes later and together we drive the cars back to my home and on the way we celebrate by stopping at the ice cream shop and getting ice cream cones to go.

I enjoy every bite of my cone and say out loud, thank you, thank you, thank you for this wonderful blessing. I know that this world has brought this wonderful car to me, I will take good care of it and I know that it will function well for me as it came to me as a special blessing.

Purchasing A New Dress

The premise for this process is that a friend is getting married and I want to purchase a new dress.

Details:

* I have looked on-line and can't find a dress because styles have changed and none of them look good on me

* My budget is $30

* I want a blue dress that matches my eyes

Senses:

* Hear myself saying that I have found the perfect dress

* See myself wearing the dress and how fantastic I look in it

* Smell the perfume I will wear with the dress and how fantastic I look in it

* Feel how good I feel while wearing the dress

* Run my hands over the material of the dress and it is so soft

Emotions and Energy:

* Excited that I finally found the dress

* Thrilled because I look great in it

The mini movie I'll play:

> I am home and the phone rings. I answer it and find out it is my Avon lady calling.

> We chit chat for a few minutes about her business, kids, and grandchildren. We talk about my business and my family. We have known each other for almost 20 years. How the time flies.

> I thank her for the fabulous customer service she has always given me. She has not only been my Avon lady but a friend.

> She asks if I need anything and I say, "No, I'm good for now but thank you so much for calling."

> We chat a little longer and I mention that I going out to the store yet again to find this dress that I've been hunting for and she says, "I have a dress in my overstock. I believe it is your size, I think you'll love the style. I think it'll look great on you. Let me check."

> She checks and comes back on the line and says, "Yes I still have it and it is your size."

> She continues to describe the dress to me and I realize that she is correct, the style is perfect for me and it is even the perfect length.

> I expectantly ask her, "What color is it?" She says, "It is blue. Actually it is the color of your eyes."

I ask cautiously, "How much is the dress." And I can't believe I'm hearing her correctly when she says, "It was a clearance item and it is $20 plus tax."

I'm so excited! Then she says, "I'll be your area tomorrow. Can you leave me a check and I'll leave the dress between your doors that way you'll have a few days to shop for the just the right shoes?"

I hear myself, "Of course and thank you, again, so much for calling me and making this happen. I am so excited!"

I am elated. I can't believe that I just found the perfect dress for me and I didn't even have to leave my house.

I call my best friend and tell her how I just found the perfect dress and I am so excited.

I see myself the next day coming home from work, opening up the package and marveling at how soft the material is when I run my fingers over it. I can't wait to try it on.

I walk quickly down the hall to my bedroom and excitedly change into the dress and it fits perfectly. Actually, I look 15 pounds slimmer in it and yes, it is the exact color of my eyes.

I am so excited I must spray a little perfume on just to revel in the moment of how great I look in my new dress.   I again run my hands down the sides of the dress so I can feel the softness of the material.

I am ecstatic over finding my new dress and I am so thankful that I found it through my Avon lady doing what she does best, giving great customer service.

I am so thankful for having her in my life.   She comes through for me all of the time.   She has become a very good friend over the years.

It is amazing as I think about my life and many of the wonderful people that I have been blessed to know.

I truly am blessed and thankful for such a life as mine.

Journal

If you are someone that keeps a journal, fantastic; keep it up and add your work on this material to it. If not, then you need to start.

The reason for keeping the journal is so that you can track when the idea came to you about something that you desired. You can keep notes about what you were going to focus on to make the desire come to you.

Most importantly, it is a record that you focused and were asking for something. And then, when your desire showed up in your life, you need to journal that as well. That is really important to document.

Here's why. This is the evidence of your asking and receiving. This evidence being written down is now concrete and something that your conscious mind now can take in and say, yes, I did ask and yes, it did come.

It will show your conscious mind just how powerful you are as a person and that you know how to use your subconscious mind to make any changes you want in your life.

The second reason is that we often forget that we have asked for something. This would be me. Time would go by and one of my desires would just show up. I used to think that it just happened, just because. I thought it was a coincidence until I learned differently. As said earlier, there are no coincidences in this world. Everything happens for a reason.

I kept asking for things to happen in my life and my life kept getting better and better, but I didn't put it together that it was because I had asked. I knew in my heart, but not in my mind that my thoughts were creating my life and that this world was creating the life I was asking for.

For me, it was finally when other people around me reminded me that I had shared my desires with them and when they showed up I excitedly shared the news with them and they would say, WOW, you manifested that; remember when we talked about that. What a wake-up call for me.

So, please, don't be like me and not keep that journal. The more you journal and affirm that your thoughts brought about the creations in this world for you, the better and better you will get at manifesting the life that you want. After all, isn't that what we all want?

Good Luck and Additional Tips

If you get nothing else from this book besides this, it will be worth the time you spent to read this book to learn that the thoughts that you are thinking are creating the life that you are living.

I can't stress this enough. Please pay attention to your thoughts.

In working with the desires that you have, remember to find your driving force where your power comes from. Embrace it, understand it and use it. You will fly!

Reminder: You don't need to know the how so don't get stuck on it. You just need to remember once you have done the process the next step is in knowing that it is coming and not questioning it.

You are in control of your life. You are always in control. Don't forget this. You can change your life.

Your past doesn't matter; it doesn't have to define you. If you are stuck, you can get unstuck.

If you have been focusing on something and believe that you hit the mark of the 68 seconds and you don't have it yet, then go ahead and repeat the process. It can't hurt.

The more focus you give to it, the faster it will show up. Even if you don't get to the 68 seconds, the more repetition, the better. This is putting the desire out in front of all of your thoughts and it is building that belief

– it is becoming stronger and stronger and it will show up.

Another belief to remember is that this desire of yours is right in front of you. If it were not, you would not have it coming up for you as a burning desire to be fulfilled. It is YOUR desire.

Remember, the manifesting of this desire doesn't have to be difficult, include a lot hard work, be time-consuming or costly. It can be effortless, BUT, it will be however you think it is going to be. I caution you to check your thoughts.

What will you do with the rest of the time that you have to make a difference in this world? Will all of your desires be for your benefit or do you want to truly make a difference in this world for this world?

I would like to share another habit that I have in my life that I believe puts and keeps me in a great place and has blessed me more than I could have ever dreamed of or wished for.

Every morning when my alarm rings, I push the snooze button, which gives me another 5 minutes.

I spend those 5 minutes thinking about everything in my life that comes to mind that I am thankful and grateful for and I either say them to myself or I'll say them out loud.

I continue this process until my alarm rings again and then I wrap up my thankfulness and gratefulness time.

Now, when I step onto the floor, first thing in the morning, I am in a wonderful place, giving off very high energy and very thankful that I have the rest of this day to make a difference for this world.

I wish and want the very best this life has to offer you and I hope that you will use the ideas and processes I have offered to change your life to make it be the life of your dreams.

So dream big, why not?

Thank you

My goal is to make a huge difference for this world one person at a time. Together we can accomplish or change anything. We can focus on desires that will change this world as well as change things for ourselves.

I want you to really reach for the sky and find for yourself what is here for you.

I am honored every morning when I am given the greatest gift I could be given: the gift of another day to make a difference.

Please feel free to contact me at 68secondspark@gmail.com.

the
68
SECOND
SPARK

shift your focus, shift your life

Karen Marie

www.ingramcontent.com/pod-product-compliance
Lightning Source LLC
Chambersburg PA
CBHW071103040426
42443CB00013B/3385